A Thames Valley line-up at Reading General station, showing typical Tilling group purchases of the 1950s. They all have Bristol chassis and Eastern Coach Works (ECW) bodies and are, from the left: a 1947 L6B that was rebuilt to 30ft length in 1957 with a Gardner 5LW engine and fitted with a new 39-seat body; a 1954 LS6B (underfloor-mounted Bristol AVW engine) with 41-seat body; and a late-model (1952) LWL6B, 30ft long and 8ft wide, with 39-seat body.
P. R. Wallis

Ian ALLAN Publishing

THE HEYDAY OF
THE CLASSIC BUS
GAVIN BOOTH

First published 1994
Third impression 1996

ISBN 0 7110 2227 5

© Ian Allan Ltd, 1994

Published by Ian Allan Publishing
an imprint of Ian Allan Ltd, Terminal House,
Station Approach, Shepperton, Surrey TW17 8AS;
and printed by Ian Allan Printing Ltd,
Coombelands House, Coombelands Lane,
Addlestone, Weybridge, Surrey KT15 1HY

Front cover:
A typical municipal bus of the early postwar
period, still in service in the 1960s, this is a
1947 Maidstone Corporation Daimler CVG6
with 56-seat Northern Coachbuilders
bodywork, painted in the undertaking's
unusual brown and cream livery. In pursuit are
two Maidstone & District Leylands – an MCW-
bodied Atlantean and a Leyland-bodied Titan
PD2. They are seen in July 1965, when the
Daimler was quite elderly and relegated to peak
duties, in Bishop's Way, passing the M&D
'Omnibus Station'.
M. J. Russell

Back cover:
Douglas Corporation, on the Isle of Man, was
an enthusiastic AEC buyer and built up a fleet
of Regents of various types. This Regent V was
one of two delivered in 1965 with Willowbrook
64-seat forward-entrance bodywork; it is seen at
Victoria Pier in Douglas in June 1975. Douglas
Corporation's motorbuses lasted until they were
acquired by the Manx Government and merged
into the Isle of Man Road Services fleet; the
Corporation still runs the famous horse trams
on Douglas promenades.
M. J. Russell

Introduction

It was obvious to me from the start that the terms 'Heyday' and 'Classic Bus' had to be
subjective. For many who are interested in buses, the heyday probably coincides with the
years when they were first developing that interest. It certainly did in my case, and so this
book covers the 1950s and 1960s.

It concentrates on motorbuses in what tended to be called 'the provinces', a term that
always seemed patronising to those of us living there, and is a companion to the books The
Heyday of London's Buses *and* The Heyday of the Tram; *as a result, London buses are not*
covered, except as second-hand purchases, and coaches will be fully covered in a later book
in the series. The only coaches that creep in are coach-seated vehicles in use on service bus
duties.

The 1950s started out well for the UK bus industry. Passenger carryings had reached
peak levels in the late 1940s, before private motoring came within the grasp of a large
proportion of the population, and before television changed evening travel habits.

After the shortages of the early postwar years, operators were at last beginning to take
delivery of substantial numbers of new buses, and these were the buses they really wanted,
rather than the assortment they were often forced to buy in the 1940s. Manufacturers were
able to concentrate on producing proper postwar models, where for some years necessity
forced them to offer what were effectively updated prewar designs. There were exciting
innovations: underfloor-engines allowed up to 45 passengers in a 30ft long single-decker;
bigger engines and more forgiving gearboxes featured in double-deckers; and the newly-
nationalised Bristol company was developing a revolutionary model that would influence
double-deck design for the next few decades.

Soon there was a clamour for lighter-weight, higher-capacity buses, as passenger
numbers started on what has proved to be a steady decline, and operators sought to
economise. This produced popular single-deckers like the AEC Reliance and Leyland Tiger
Cub, and double-deck bodies like the MCW Orion that weighed little more than two tons,
but could accommodate up to 66 passengers.

Then came demands for longer and wider buses. Double-deckers could be 30ft long on
two axles from 1956, and 36ft single-deckers were legalised from 1961. These changes led
to new models like Leyland's rear-engined Atlantean double-decker and its close rival, the
Daimler Fleetline, and to a rash of rear-engined single-deckers, not all of which were
particularly successful.

Previous page:
Restrictions on new bus deliveries during World War 2 and vehicle shortages in the early postwar period meant that many older buses continued in service long after they would normally have been withdrawn. The AEC Regent was a popular double-deck chassis, and its main competitors for municipal business were models from Crossley, Daimler and Leyland. This Brighton Corporation Regent with 56-seat Weymann bodywork was one of 10 supplied in 1939. It is seen at Brighton's Old Steine in August 1960. With the preservation movement beginning to gain momentum at the time, many of the long-lived buses of the 1960s were saved; sister vehicle FUF 63 survives.
Arnold Richardson/Photobus

Right:
Several operators turned to rebuilding and rebodying to prolong the lives of their buses, and in 1958 the Derby-based Trent company had 20 of these 1947 AEC Regals rebuilt by Willowbrook as 30ft long 39-seat dual-purpose vehicles. The AEC Regal was one of the most popular of the front-engined chassis that quickly became outmoded in the 1950s with the arrival of underfloor-engined models, and full-width fronts and concealed radiators were typical attempts to disguise the age of the bus. Alongside, in this 1960 Matlock view, is a 1938 North Western Bristol L5G that had been rebodied by Burlingham in 1950 and which lasted in service until 1963.
Arnold Richardson/Photobus

The size and structure of the UK bus industry at the time means that in fewer than 90 photographs it is impossible to cover all operators, even all the major operators. There is an attempt at geographical equality, but often the availability and quality of the photographs dictated what was included. If your favourite operator isn't included, I'm sorry; the only consolation I can offer is that mine isn't either. The emphasis, therefore, is on the vehicles, and the book presents a representative selection of the types of bus that operated in the UK in the 1950s and 1960s; this includes buses from the 1930s and 1940s that were still in service, and buses bought new.

Most of the buses in the UK fell into five main categories: there was London Transport with 7,743 motorbuses, 96 municipal operators with 16,892, 35 British Electric Traction (BET) group companies with 11,783, 38 British Transport Commission companies (the Tilling and Scottish groups) with 15,107, and a large number of independents, including such giants as West Riding (447), Lancashire United Transport (392) and Barton Transport (268) – figures from the 1959 Passenger Transport Year Book.

There were also several thousand trolleybuses in service, including over 1,600 with London Transport – with other sizeable operators including Belfast, Bournemouth, Bradford, Derby, Glasgow, Newcastle, Nottingham, Reading, Walsall and Wolverhampton – and 1,274 electric trams still operated on six systems (Blackpool, Glasgow, Grimsby & Immingham, Leeds, Sheffield and Swansea & Mumbles) on the mainland along with the three lines on the Isle of Man. But outside Blackpool, urban electric trams would all be gone by 1962, and the trolleybuses would gradually dwindle over the next dozen years.

The structure of the industry remained very stable during the 1950s and 1960s. The control of the nationalised bus companies passed from the British Transport Commission to the Transport Holding Co in 1963, but the end of that same decade heralded massive changes that saw the BET group selling out to THC and creating the National Bus Co, the creation of the Scottish Bus Group, the formation of the first Passenger Transport Authorities, and the hiving-off of London Transport's Country Area operations to create London Country. On the manufacturing side, Leyland swallowed up all its competition to hold a virtual monopoly on bus supplies. It was the start of a period of change that never seems to have finished.

This book then represents the last of the old order, arguably the last age of innocence. Many of the operators represented in these pages have disappeared – some have gone out of business, others have been merged into larger groupings and PTEs, still others survive but under different names. Most of the liveries have changed, and while some colours still survive, they are usually applied in quite different ways.

The photographs came from a selection of photographers who were taking quality colour work in this period. It seems that many photographers turned to colour transparencies in the 1970s, but few were active before this. Most pictures date from the 1960s – there are some from the 1950s, and a couple slip into the 1970s depicting earlier vehicles. They were chosen with great difficulty from an encouragingly large selection of good material, and some of those that were squeezed out will be used in the bi-monthly magazine Classic Bus.

Enjoy this colourful return to the heyday of the bus.

September 1993

Gavin Booth
Edinburgh

AEC introduced its improved Regent III double-deck model in 1947, and this sophisticated, smooth-running chassis became popular with municipal, company and independent fleets throughout the UK and overseas. Glasgow Corporation had a policy of buying its new buses from several sources, which was particularly important in the early postwar period when manufacturers were being encouraged to export, and home operators had to shop around for buses to carry the record passenger numbers. This 1948 Regent III, seen at Anniesland in May 1961, was one of 20 with Northern Coachbuilders 56-seat bodywork.
Iain MacGregor

London Transport buses were always popular second-hand purchases, reflecting LT's high specification and the strict maintenance methods. Until more recent times, London buses tended only to appear on the second-hand market after a long spell in the capital, but non-standard types have occasionally been prematurely sold, like the 120 AEC Regent RT types bodied by Craven in 1948-50. These were eagerly snapped up by a range of operators when they were sold after just seven year's service, and the well-known Scottish independent operator, McGills of Barrhead, bought this example from another Scottish independent in 1960. Painted in the attractive McGills livery, the former RT1438 is seen in Renfrew in May 1962 in the company of Leylands from the fleets of Garners and Patons, two more of the famous Paisley area independents of which only McGills survives today.
Iain MacGregor

New double-deckers were regularly bought by smaller independent operators, and West Wales Motors, of Ammanford, bought a succession of new buses like this 1950 AEC Regent III with Weymann lowbridge bodywork, seen in Ammanford in July 1963 in the unusual grey, red and cream livery. This combination of AEC Regent and Weymann bodywork was also chosen by London Transport when it bought its RLH class in 1950-52. The lowbridge body layout, with its offside sunken gangway on the upper deck, was the solution for many operators looking to run higher-capacity buses on services with low railway bridges. The introduction of the Bristol Lodekka allowed nationalised fleets to move to a more conventional double-deck layout, but other operators had to wait for more generally available models. West Wales dabbled with some of these, but without great success.
P. R. Wallis

Eastbourne Corporation claims to have
operated the world's first municipal bus service,
in 1903; the town was unusual in that it
decided not to operate electric tramcars. This
Eastbourne AEC Regent III, seen in July 1970
in Seaside (the name of the road), was one of
eight bought in 1951 with bodies by East
Lancashire Coachbuilders which were finished
by Bruce Coachworks. The Regent III was
AEC's standard double-deck model until 1954,
when a demand for lighter-weight buses
produced the Regent V. The Regent IV never
went into production; it was an experimental
underfloor-engined double-deck chassis.
M. J. Russell

AEC's first underfloor-engined single-deck model was the Regal Mk IV, a heavyweight chassis featuring a horizontal version of the 9.6 litre engine from the Regal III and Regent III chassis. London Transport was the main home market customer for the Regal IV, with the 715-strong RF family, and many were chosen for coaching work. Scottish Omnibuses bought 34 30-seaters with toilets for Edinburgh-London coach services in 1951-53, and also took 10 40-seaters for more general work. One of these, with Alexander bodywork, is seen on a local service in Edinburgh's St Andrew Square, complete with the inevitable paper sticker augmenting the destination display. Scottish Omnibuses, which continued to trade as SMT, was the parent company of what became the Scottish Bus Group, nationalised in 1949 as part of the British Transport Commission.
J. T. Inglis

Far left:
Although most operators quickly switched to underfloor-engined chassis when these became available, some, like Doncaster Corporation, stuck to the older front-engined models. This Yorkshire municipality bought three of these AEC Regal III with Roe 39-seat bodies in 1953. The combination of the classic AEC radiator and the subtle lines of the Roe bodywork resulted in a most attractive bus, seen here in 1969. This bus is now preserved.
M. Fowler

Above left:
AEC introduced its lighter-weight Reliance chassis in 1953, and this was to remain a popular choice with operators until 1979. The Reliance was equally at home as a bus or a coach, and was bought by a wide range of companies in the UK and overseas. This 1957 example, with Willowbrook bodywork, seen leaving Bishop Auckland in August 1965 on a service to West Hartlepool with a respectable load, was owned by Gillett Bros of Ferryhill, one of the plethora of independents serving this part of County Durham.
Geoffrey Morant/Photobus

Below left:
Baxters Bus Services of Airdrie, one of Scotland's best-loved independents, ran a smart fleet of blue-painted buses in the Airdrie and Coatbridge areas of Lanarkshire. This 1956 AEC Reliance had Alexander 41-seat bodywork of a style most commonly associated with Scottish Bus Group fleets. Baxters sold out to Scottish Omnibuses in 1962, but when the Baxters buses started to appear in SOL green, local resistance led the company to revive the name and the livery for another 15 years. More recently the livery made a shortlived reappearance on Kelvin Central's Monklands Bus operation.
J. Thomson

Above:
After many years as an all-trolleybus fleet, Ipswich Corporation bought its first motorbuses in 1950. This AEC Regent III was one of four with Park Royal 61-seat bodies bought in 1956, and is seen in October 1971 at Whitton terminus. The Electric House name for the city centre terminus is a reminder of the trolleybus operation. This particularly attractive style of Park Royal four-bay bodywork was chosen by several municipal and company operators in the mid-1950s. A similar bus is preserved.
M. J. Russell

Right:
For many years double-deckers in the East Yorkshire fleet had bodies with roofs shaped to pass under the 15th century North Bar at Beverley. This resulted in most distinctive bodies with a pronounced inward lean at upper-deck window level, and an exaggerated roof dome. This is a 1956 AEC Regent V with an exposed radiator rather than the enclosed front that graced most examples of this model. The 56-seat 'Beverley Bar' bodywork is by Willowbrook, and the bus is seen in Queen Victoria Square, Hull in May 1971.
M. J. Russell

Far left:
In contrast to a Regent V with an exposed radiator, this tin-front AEC is actually a Regent III with lowbridge MCW Orion 55-seat bodywork, one of nine delivered in 1956 to the Sheffield Corporation 'B' fleet. It is seen at Pond Street bus station, Sheffield, in April 1970. Under the Sheffield Corporation umbrella there were three similarly-liveried fleets, a consequence of the powers obtained by railway companies in 1928 to operate bus services. The LMS and LNER railway companies set up the Sheffield Joint Omnibus Committee with the Corporation. The Sheffield 'A' fleet was entirely Corporation-owned, operating within the city; the 'B' fleet was jointly owned with the railways for services to intermediate points outside the city; and the 'C' fleet was entirely railway owned, operating long-distance services. The railway involvement meant that during the nationalised years, Bristol and ECW products could be bought for the 'B' and 'C' fleets; in practice some ECW bodies were bought, but mounted on Leyland chassis. These arrangements lasted until 1970.
Policy Transport Photographs

A late-model AEC Regent III from the Reading Corporation fleet, with Park Royal 56-seat lowbridge bodywork. Reading was one of a number of municipalities that required lowbridge and eventually lowheight buses. This example is seen in Station Road freshly outshopped after overhaul in September 1971.
M. J. Russell

Above:
AEC's first attempt at a lowheight bus in the Bristol Lodekka mould was the Bridgemaster, developed by its associated company, Crossley. This was one of the earliest Bridgemasters, demonstrator 76 MME, which came to rest with Barton Transport, the famous independent operator, after its demonstration tour. It was new in 1957 with Crossley 72-seat bodywork,

and is seen at Peterborough bus station in September 1971.
Policy Transport Photographs

Right:
Unpainted finishes were briefly fashionable in the 1950s as a means of saving the costs of painting. Several large operators bought examples, but all of these succumbed to the

paintbrush in time. This South Wales 30ft long AEC Regent V was one of 13 unpainted examples from a batch of 33 delivered in 1958/59. It has Weymann forward-entrance 71-seat bodywork, and is seen in Llanelli in July 1963.
P. R. Wallis

Left:
The lightweight MCW Orion body was a popular purchase for municipal and company operators in the 1950s and 1960s, though observers have widely different views about its aesthetic appeal. One livery which did much to disguise the Orion was that of St Helens Corporation, which bought eight of these 64-seat AEC Regent V in 1962. One is seen in Corporation Street in April 1973.
M. J. Russell

Above:
Albion, owned by Leyland Motors since 1951, continued to develop and build a wide range of bus and truck chassis. One model that was moderately successful was the Nimbus, an underfloor-engined chassis to what would today be regarded as midi length. This Guernsey Railway NS3AN model of 1961 was one of 15 of the type bought between 1961 and 1965 for work on the island. The somewhat vintage looking bodywork was by Reading of

Portsmouth, and had seats for 35. It is seen at St Peter Port in 1967.
Policy Transport Photographs

19

Far left:
A classic bus if ever there was one: the Bedford OB with Duple Vista body that was so familiar throughout the UK in the 1950s, and which can still be seen, both on special vintage services, and at rallies, for there are literally dozens preserved. It was the mainstay of many country services, and although attempts were made to produce a replacement chassis, nothing quite achieved the success of the OB. This 1950 29-seater is seen in service with Pioneer (D. H. Roberts) of Newport, Pembrokeshire, in July 1963 at Goodwick.
P. R. Wallis

Above left:
Before Bedford introduced the VAS model, operators requiring smaller chassis could specify an adaptation of the J series goods model. This 1960 J4LZ1 with Duple 16-seat body, was used by the Sutherland Transport & Trading Co Ltd on its mailbus services in the north of Scotland. The low seating capacity is explained by the sizeable mail compartment that was a feature of the Sutherland Transport and David MacBrayne buses, which provided a combined bus/mail service to the more remote communities in the Highlands. This bus is seen at Lochinver in June 1963.
R. L. Wilson

Below left:
The giant Birmingham & Midland Motor Omnibus Co, better known as Midland Red, built its own buses and coaches for many years, and was noted for its advanced designs. Its last sizeable 'home-made' double-deck model was the 30ft long D9, and 345 were built between 1958 and 1966. The D9 was integrally constructed, with rubber suspension, independent on the front axle, power steering, and an all-hydraulic braking system. A 1961 example is seen in Birmingham in 1963 in the unrelieved red livery used by the company. An illuminated advertisement panel, a fashion of the time, is fitted. Midland Red built two experimental D10 underfloor-engined double-deckers, but moved on to Daimler Fleetlines for its next generation vehicles.
Arnold Richardson/Photobus

Above:

During World War 2 new bus building was strictly controlled, and vehicles were released to customers based on need. The wartime utility specification called for very basic buses with the minimum of frills, though by the end of the war a more relaxed specification was being applied. A late surviving utility-style bus was this Colchester Corporation 1945 Bristol K6A with Park Royal 56-seat bodywork. It survived in service until 1965 in largely unrebuilt form, which was rare for buses of this age.

A. J. Douglas/Photobus

Right:

Bristol chassis and Eastern Coach Works bodies became the staple diet for Tilling group companies after nationalisation in 1948. The other nationalised fleets – London Transport and the Scottish Bus Group – could buy Bristol and/or ECW products as well as proprietary models, and both exercised this right. The main models for many years were the single-deck L and double-deck K, which had their chassis designations altered as they grew longer and wider. This Western National K6A, with AEC engine, has ECW 55-seat lowbridge bodywork,

of a style that was familiar in many parts of the country. The front dome in this August 1965 scene at the Stoke Gabriel terminus of route 178 from Paignton shows the scars from low-hanging trees. These were the days when village bus routes were still worked by two-man double-deckers.

M. J. Russell

Although the Tilling group companies were
enthusiastic Bristol/ECW buyers before
nationalisation, the combination was also
favoured by other fleets. This L5G was one of
three with ECW 35-seat rear-entrance

bodywork supplied to Merthyr Tydfil
Corporation in 1946. It is seen at its garage in
June 1963, surrounded by East Lancs-bodied
Leyland Titans.
P. R. Wallis

West Yorkshire was one of the 'red' Tilling fleets, based in Harrogate, and operating in west and north Yorkshire. This is a 1951 Bristol LL5G with ECW 39-seat body at Harrogate bus station in August 1965. The LL version of the chassis was 30ft long, and was built in 1950/51. The fleet number code SGL signifies Single-deck, Gardner (engine), Long.
G. W. Dickson

25

Below:
Following the relaxation of vehicle dimensions, Bristol introduced the 27ft x 8ft KSW chassis in 1950, and over 1,000 were built until production ceased in 1957; all had ECW bodywork. This KSW5G (Gardner 5LW engine) with lowbridge 55-seat body was one of 54 supplied to Wilts & Dorset in 1951-53. It is seen at Salisbury bus station in 1966, with a Bristol LS at the rear.
I. Parish

Right:
The highbridge Bristol KSW was an impressive beast. Bristol Omnibus and its associated companies built up a large fleet, and this Cheltenham District KWS6G was one of a small number of buses throughout the Tilling group that were not painted in standard Tilling green or red liveries. ECW 60-seat bodywork was fitted to this late (1956) example, seen at St Mark's Road, Cheltenham in April 1972.
M. J. Russell

Far left:
The first Bristol/ECW underfloor-engined single-deck model was the semi-integral LS, built from 1950 to 1958 in both bus and coach form. Although many Tilling fleets took examples of the distinctive coach body for long-distance and touring work, some also took the bus body shell, fitted coach-type seats, and used them on longer bus services. This United Automobile Services example is a 1957 LS6B (Bristol engine) with 39-seat dual-purpose body, and is seen at Valley Bridge, Scarborough in August 1965.
G. H. F. Atkins

Above left:
The Bristol/ECW solution to the need for lightweight rural buses was the front-engined SC, normally with Gardner 4LK engine. It was in production from 1955 to 1961, and nine of the more rural Tilling fleets bought a total of 323. Crosville was a good SC customer, and this example has ECW 35-seat bodywork.
D. Kerrison/Photobus

Below left:
Bristol's successor to the semi-integral LS was the MW chassis, introduced in 1957 and in production for 10 years; nearly 2,000 were built. This was Red & White's first MW, and one of the very first built, in 1957. It is an MW5G model with ECW 45-seat bodywork. The Red & White numbering system made it easy to date their buses; U157 was the first underfloor-engined bus bought in 1957. It is seen in August 1965.
Roy Marshall/Photobus

Far left:
The Bristol / ECW Lodekka has proved to be one of the most significant double-deck bus designs of the postwar period. The designers produced a bus with a drop-centre rear axle, which allowed a sunken lower deck gangway, and normal upper deck seating within the 'lowbridge' overall height of 13ft 6in. The original 27ft long LD model was in production from 1953 to 1961, and 2,179 were were built for the nationalised Tilling and Scottish fleets. This early LD5G model was supplied to Eastern National in 1954, with a 58-seat body. It is seen in Southend-on-Sea on what was evidently a hot day in May 1971.
M. J. Russell

Above left:
The F (flat floor) series Bristol Lodekka models replaced the LD series in most fleets from 1959. These had a proper flat floor and air suspension. The ECW body was subtly updated, and looks well in the attractive red and cream livery of Brighton Hove & District. This 1960 FS6B 60-seater is seen in Brighton when new.
Arnold Richardson/Photobus

Below left:
Replacing the mid-size SC model was the underfloor-engined SU, with an Albion 4-cylinder engine. Available in short and long wheelbase variants, the SU remained in production from 1960 until 1966, and 181 were built. Most were the longer SUL4A model with ECW 36-seat bodywork and this was one of a number supplied to the associated Southern and Western National fleets. It was new to Southern National in 1965.
I. Parish

The F series Lodekka was built in forward-entrance variations, and the shorter FSF, built between 1960 and 1963, was one of the less common versions; only 218 were built. This 1962 FSF6G with 60-seat body was one of a sizeable batch for the United Welsh fleet. It is seen in Llanelly in July 1963.

32   P. R. Wallis

Another of the non-standard Tilling liveries was the attractive blue used by Notts & Derby. This 1965 Bristol Lodekka FLF6G model with ECW 70-seat forward entrance body was typical of many supplied to Tilling and Scottish fleets until 1968. It is seen in June 1965. Of the total 5,217 Lodekkas built, 1,867 were FLFs.
R. L. Wilson

33

Left:
Crossley chassis were familiar in several large fleets in the early postwar period. The double-deck model, the DD42, was built between 1946 and 1953, and though some were withdrawn prematurely, they soldiered on in other fleets. This 1949 DD42/7 was one of a batch of six supplied to Cardiff Corporation with Alexander lowbridge 53-seat bodies. It was still in service in July 1963, here at Cardiff bus station. A similar bus is preserved.
P. R. Wallis

Above:
Luton Corporation was another Crossley user, and this DD42 with lowbridge Crossley 53-seat body, was one of 12 built in 1948. The Crossley bodywork has echoes of the streamlined designs produced for Manchester Corporation, an enthusiastic Crossley user for many years. Luton Corporation was an early municipal casualty, selling out to United Counties in 1970. This photograph was taken in April 1963.
P. R. Wallis

Right:
For many years Daimler buses were particularly associated with municipal fleets, where the preselective transmission made for easier driving in urban traffic. Daimler was allowed to continue building double-deck chassis during World War 2, even though its factories suffered badly in the bombing of Coventry, and London Transport received 281 CW series chassis between 1944 and 1946. When new buses reached London in sufficient quantities many were sold on for further service, and Belfast Corporation bought 66 in 1953/54, which were rebodied by local builder, Harkness, in 1955/56 and gave good service for some years. This rebodied former London vehicle is seen in the centre of Belfast in December 1965.
A. J. Douglas/Photobus

Far right:
SHMD was a more convenient way of describing the Stalybridge, Hyde, Mossley and Dukinfield Transport & Electricity Board, operating to the east of Manchester. SHMD was a dedicated Daimler user, and this 1949 CVD6 was one of 10 with East Lancs 56-seat bodywork. It is seen in July 1958.
D. Kerrison/Photobus

Left:
Birmingham City Transport had built up a substantial Daimler fleet in the prewar years, and continued to favour the Daimler/MCW combination in the postwar period. This CVD6, one of 100 supplied in 1949 with MCW 54-seat bodywork to Birmingham's solid, but somewhat

dated, design, is seen in August 1963 in Albert Street, Birmingham.
G. W. Dickson

Above:
Daimler adopted the style of enclosed bonnet first developed by Birmingham City Transport

as its standard 'new look' front in the 1950s. This Swindon Corporation CVG6, seen in Milton Road in September 1973, has Park Royal 61-seat bodywork, one of 24 supplied in 1956/57.
M. J. Russell

Daimler's underfloor-engined chassis, the Freeline, was firmly in the heavyweight league, and the company never developed an equivalent of the highly successful lighter-weight AEC Reliance and Leyland Tiger Cub models. Many were bodied as coaches, but Great Yarmouth Corporation bought three Freelines for bus work in 1962 and a further four two years later.

This was one of the 1964 buses, with Roe 43-seat body, and is pictured at Britannia Pier in August 1966.
Gavin Booth

Daimler later simplified its enclosed radiator design, and adopted a style first developed for Manchester Corporation. This Derby Corporation CVG6 with Roe 65-seat body was one of Derby's last batch of CVG6s, delivered in 1965. It is seen at the Morledge, Derby, in June 1970.

Policy Transport Photographs

41

Left:
Daimler's response to the rear-engined Leyland Atlantean model was the Fleetline, introduced in 1962, and destined to prove one of the company's best-selling chassis. The Fleetline widened Daimler's customer base, which had largely consisted of municipal operators; now Daimlers were bought by company fleets throughout the country and, with less operational success, by London Transport. This CRG6LX with East Lancs 75-seat body was one of 22 similar buses supplied to Coventry Corporation in 1966. Although Coventry, Daimler's home town, had a predominantly Daimler fleet, it also bought Leyland Atlanteans, which predictably caused a local political storm.
A. J. Varley

Above:
The widespread use of Dennis buses is a relatively recent development, and for many years the company built for a small group of customers. The most faithful was Aldershot & District, based close to the Dennis factory in Guildford. This was a 1949 Lancet III with Strachan 32-seat rear-entrance bus body, one of 23 supplied that year. It is seen at Farnborough in September 1957.
N. C. Simmons

43

Left:
The independent Lancashire United company was an occasional Dennis user, and in 1949 bought ten of these Lance K2 models with Weymann 53-seat lowbridge bodies. No 420, freshly repainted, stands outside Swinton depot in July 1963.
A. J. Douglas/Photobus

Above:
Dennis made an unsuccessful foray into the lightweight underfloor single-deck market with the Pelican model in 1954. One chassis was bodied, by Duple, but the model was then abandoned. The Pelican was bought by the independent operator, Chiltern Queens of Woodcote, with whom it is seen at Reading in

September 1963. The body was later transferred to an AEC Reliance.
P. R. Wallis

Right:
Dennis acquired the rights to build Bristol's trend-setting Lodekka under licence, but delays in getting into production meant that orders were disappointing. An unusual customer for the Loline was City of Oxford, whose fleet was heavily AEC-dominated, although the Oxford Lolines did at least have AEC engines. This 1960 Loline II, seen in April 1963, had East Lancs 63-seat bodywork, and is seen in Oxford's distinctive livery. A similar bus is preserved.
P. R. Wallis

Below right:
Foden had dabbled in bus-building before World War 2, but entered the postwar market with enthusiasm, offering the first commercially-available chassis with full-width fronts. These echoed the fronts on contemporary Foden trucks, and attracted operators looking to present a more modern image. There were two main models – the PVSC single-deck and PVD double-deck, which were both sturdy front-engined chassis – and these were on the market from 1946 until 1956. From 1950 Foden also offered the PVR, a rear-engined bus/coach chassis, which predated the 1960s trend to rear-emergined vehicles, but it was not a great success. This PVSC6 with Plaxton 33-seat body was used by Strachan's Deeside Omnibus Service of Ballater for its services to Aberdeen, where it is seen in the early 1960s.
Peter Tulloch

Far right:
Warrington Corporation was the most enthusiastic Foden double-deck customer and in 1956 bought five of these PVD6 with East Lancs 58-seat bodies. These were among the last Foden buses to be built at that time. It is seen late in its life returning to Wilderspool Causeway depot. Foden returned to the double-deck market with a rear-engined double-decker in 1976, a possible alternative to the Daimler Fleetline, but this never really progressed beyond the prototype stage.

46   M. J. Russell

Left:
Guy, a low volume bus builder in the prewar years, was suddenly thrust into the front line when it was selected to build utility double-deck chassis during World War 2. Nearly 3,000 Arab I/II models were built between 1942 and 1946, and the rugged construction meant that many survived well into the postwar period, often rebuilt or rebodied. This Park Royal bodied Arab II was new to Southdown in 1945, but when photographed in Rhos-on-Sea in August

1957 was operating for the Llandudno & Colwyn Bay Railway Co, a shortlived bus operation between the withdrawal of the narrow-gauge trams in 1956 and the take-over by Crosville in 1961.
D. Kerrison/Photobus

Above:
After the war, Guy developed its range with the Arab III model, built between 1946 and 1953. This was a successful chassis, bought by many

of the operators who had first experienced Guys when they were allocated during the wartime years. Southampton Corporation was an enthusiastic Guy user, buying a substantial fleet of these Park Royal bodied buses between 1948 and 1954. This is a 1950 example.
M. J. Russell

Left:
Blue-painted municipal fleets were outnumbered by the more familiar reds and greens, but Birkenhead Corporation used this attractive blue and cream until the fleet was absorbed into Merseyside PTE in 1969. This Guy Arab III was one of 15 with Massey 56-seat bodies delivered in 1950. Massey bodies, built in Wigan, were noted for their flowing lines and the D-shaped lower deck windows were another design feature. This scene is at Woodside Ferry in May 1964.
J. T. Inglis

Above:
Although Southdown was a committed Leyland user, it also bought Guys, and this 1948 54-seat Northern Counties bodied Arab III was one of 12. The translucent panels in the roof are noteworthy. Seen at Pool Valley, Brighton, in August 1960.
Arnold Richardson/Photobus

As with Daimler, Guy adopted the Birmingham-style new-look front for its Arab IV model, and East Kent was one of a number of BET companies to choose this model in preference to the more common AECs and Leylands. This 1957 Arab IV had Park Royal 61-seat bodywork, and was one of a number supplied in the mid-1950s. It is seen turning into Market Square, Dover in April 1968 on a Dover town service.
M. J. Russell

Some of the independents which bought new
double-deckers were Guy fans. Premier of
Stainforth took delivery of this Roe-bodied Arab
IV in 1956. It is seen at Christ Church,
Doncaster, a famous terminus for the multitude
of independents that once served the area
around the town, in May 1958.
Roger Holmes

Right:
Like Daimler, Guy's success in the underfloor-engined single-deck market was limited. This 1954 Guy-bodied Huddersfield Corporation bus is seen at the old Huddersfield Upperhead Row bus station in August 1968. It was one of seven Arab UF models owned by this undertaking. Guy offered its own bodywork for a number of years, typically built on Park Royal frames. It was nothing like as popular as the combination of Leyland bodywork on Leyland chassis.
H. J. Black

Below right:
Several operators (arguably with good reason) chose to hide the manufacturers' front-ends behind fully-enclosed fronts, which were no doubt intended to give the buses a more modern look. Wolverhampton Corporation took 30 of these 30ft Guy Arab IV with MCW 72-seat forward entrance bodies in 1961. This one is seen in 1969.
Policy Transport Photographs

Far right:
For a short period Guy offered a different front end, based on buses built for service in Johannesburg, South Africa. This Burton-on-Trent Corporation example had a Massey 61-seat body, and was one of three delivered in 1961 with Gardner 5LW engines instead of the more familiar, and more powerful, 6LW. It is seen on Burton Bridge in March 1973.

M. J. Russell

Right:
*Elderly Leylands were still to be found in many
fleets in the 1950s and 1960s, and although
many had been rebuilt and rebodied after the
war, some still looked very much as they had
been when new. This Titan TD4 model was
new to Portsmouth Corporation in 1935 and
was still in service when photographed here 28
years later, in July 1963. It had six-bay vee-
fronted Leyland bodywork with seats for only
52 passengers.*
A. J. Douglas/Photobus

Far right:
*The Leyland Cheetah was a full-size
lightweight single-deck model which found
favour with a number of operators, notably the
SMT group. This 1939 LZ2A with Alexander
39-seat body was still in largely original
condition when photographed in service with
Norfolks of Nayland in August 1963 at
Haverhill; many of its heavyweight brothers
were requisitioned for war service, and after the
war were heavily rebuilt or rebodied. Norfolks
was one of the longest-established transport
operators in East Anglia, having started with
horse-drawn vehicles in the 1850s.*
P. R. Wallis

Far left:
*The giant Alexander fleet still had a large
number of older Leylands giving good service
well into the 1960s. This 1940 Leyland Titan
TD7, with 53-seat Leyland lowbridge
bodywork, seen in Dock Street, Dundee, lasted
in service until 1962. Note the remains of the
tramlines in the cobbles, and the inevitable
conductress hanging off the rear platform. The
Alexander fleet was split into three separate
companies – Fife, Midland and Northern – in
1961.*
J. Thomson

Above left:
*To speed deliveries in the early postwar years,
several Tilling group companies took examples
of Leyland's Titan PD1A model with ECW
bodywork. This Eastern Counties example, new
in 1947, had a 53-seat lowbridge body. It is
seen in September 1959.*
R. L. Wilson

Below left:
*The Titan PD1 and the equivalent Tiger PS1
were Leyland's first new postwar models, and
were on the market from 1946 to 1951. They
had Leyland's 7.4 litre engine and a constant
mesh gearbox, and although they lacked the
sophistication of the later PD2 and PS2 models,
they proved to be useful buses at a time when
operators were desperate to restock their fleets.
This PS1 Tiger, a 1949 Western SMT example
seen in Ayr in June 1962, is typical of many
bought by SMT group companies, most with
Alexander 35-seat bodies as here.*
M. Fowler

Above:
The massive Manchester Corporation fleet included Crossleys, Daimlers and Leylands in the postwar period, many with bodies based on the streamlined design first evolved for the city's Crossleys. This 1947 Titan PD1/1 has MCW 58-seat bodywork, and is seen at Piccadilly bus station in October 1960. It was one of 50 delivered that year, which were Manchester's

first postwar Leylands. Until the late 1950s, grey roofs in Manchester indicated 7ft 6in wide buses.
Roy Marshall/Photobus

Right:
Leyland's first generally-available underfloor-engined model was sold as a complete integral vehicle, the Leyland/MCW Olympic.

Introduced in 1949, early examples were 27ft 6in long with seats for 40 passengers, and were designated HR40. This HR40 was new to King Alfred Motor Services, the famous Winchester independent in 1950; it is seen at the Winchester Broadway terminus in April 1963.
P. R. Wallis

A confirmed Leyland user, Ribble bought 30 of the longer (30ft) HR44 Olympics in 1951; the Weymann bodies seated 44. This example is seen in Windermere. British operators were unhappy about buying integral buses and Leyland responded with a separate chassis, the Royal Tiger, which sold well until the move to reduce weight produced the smaller-engined Tiger Cub. The Olympic, on the other hand, went on to spectacular sales success in export markets.
J. Thomson

Municipal operators tended to buy new buses wherever possible, but many made occasional second-hand purchases to meet certain situations. This former Leicester Corporation Leyland Titan PD2, with Leyland 56-seat bodywork, new in 1949, had been sold to Teesside Municipal Transport when photographed at North Ormesby in April 1971.

The Teesside undertaking combined the fleets of Middlesbrough and Stockton along with the Teesside Railless Traction Board and chose this unusual, and hardly flattering, turquoise and cream livery.
M. J. Russell

Left:
A truly vintage scene, with a Leyland-bodied Titan PD2 from the fleet of the independent operator Scout of Preston. Although it has all the characteristics of a recent reconstruction – cobbled streets, period cars – it was actually photographed in Preston in October 1962.
Roy Marshall/Photobus

Above:
Blackpool Corporation is best-known as a tramway operator, but it has also maintained a sizeable bus fleet, and for a while the buses had a streamlined look, which echoed the lines of the fine 1930s trams which are still in service. This Leyland Titan PD2/5, seen in July 1963, has Burlingham fully-fronted, centre-entrance

bodywork, built in Blackpool, and dates from 1948. Blackpool continued to specify full-width fronts for its double-deckers for some years, though on more conventional bodies.
A. J. Douglas/Photobus

Above:
The Tiger Cub was Leyland's solution to calls for lighter-weight underfloor-engined single-deckers. It was on the market from 1952 to 1969, and was popular in municipal, company and independent fleets. This East Midland example has Saro 44-seat bodywork, regarded by many as one of the most stylish combinations of the time. It is seen at Waterdale, Doncaster, in 1960 in the company of a Yorkshire Traction Tiger PS1 with Brush bodywork, a type once familiar in many BET group fleets, and a Crossley DD42 with Scottish Aviation body from the independent Blue Ensign fleet.
M. Fowler

Right:
London Transport's RT family Leylands tended to be sold out of service before contemporary AECs, and many operators eagerly snatched these up. Walsall Corporation bought this late-model (1954) RTL with Park Royal 56-seat bodywork, in 1959. Few operators stuck with London's exemplary destination blind information, and Walsall has reduced this to a minimum, where even the word 'WALSALL' doesn't quite fit the aperture. It is seen at Bloxwich Junction in June 1969 on morning peak relief work on trolleybus route 31, in company with one of the Walsall Sunbeam F4A/Willowbrook trolleybuses, which were the first 30ft double-deckers on two axles permitted to run in the UK.
M. J. Russell

Above:
Leyland's first 'tin front' was based on that fitted to a batch of Titan PD2s supplied to Midland Red, hence the blank space above the slots, which was for the BMMO insignia. This PD2/22 with Roe lowbridge bodywork was owned by the large independent, West Riding, which became notorious in its later years for buying most examples of the Guy Wulfrunian. A Wulfrunian with Roe body sits behind the Titan at Wakefield bus station in August 1968, and behind that an AEC Reliance/Roe, all from the West Riding fleet. The Wulfrunian had

a Gardner 6LX engine mounted on the front overhang, independent suspension and disc brakes; although the specification was advanced, the chassis was a disaster, and most examples were sold after a very short life. West Riding sold out to the Transport Holding Co in 1967.
H. J. Black

Right:
Leyland produced a lengthened version of the Titan PD2 in 1956, when regulations were relaxed to permit 30ft double-deckers on two

axles, and this was designated PD3. It was available with the Midland Red-style front, or with the traditional exposed radiator, which several operators continued to specify. This 1958 PD3/4 was delivered to Severn of Dunscroft, one of the Doncaster area independents, and was the first of six similar buses for this operator. It had a Roe 71-seat rear-entrance body, and this proved to be a most handsome combination. It is seen at Christ Church, Doncaster, in June 1963.
Roger Holmes

Above:
For many years, Jersey Motor Transport was famous for the amazing collection of vintage buses that still operated daily on the island, but in the 1960s it embarked on fleet renewal, and this Leyland Tiger Cub PSUC1/11 was one of several with short-tailed Massey bodies. It is seen on the unusual turntable at Snow Hill in 1963 bearing the almost inevitable Mary Ann beer advertisement.

M. Macklin

Right:
The West Monmouthshire Omnibus Board operated a service between Markham and Bargoed which included the notorious Bargoed Hill, with gradients peaking at around 1 in 5. Special buses were bought for this service and in 1959 West Mon bought this Leyland Titan PD2/38 (double-deck chassis) and fitted a Massey 31-seat body especially for it. As planned, the chassis eventually received a double-deck body. It is seen on a special

enthusiasts' trip in June 1963, negotiating the sharp turn under a railway bridge that was a further hazard on the route.

P. R. Wallis

Far left:
Western Welsh was an important customer for the Leyland Tiger Cub, building up a substantial fleet over a number of years. The lighter-weight Tiger Cub quickly succeeded the Royal Tiger as Leyland's principal single-deck model in this weight-obsessed era. Demands for less weight but more power led to the introduction of the Leopard in 1959, which went on to become a best-seller. This 1954 Tiger Cub PSUC1/1 with Weymann 44-seat body is seen at Goodwick in July 1963.
P. R. Wallis

Left:
Edinburgh Corporation bought 300 Leyland Titan PD2/20s in the mid-1950s to replace its tramway fleet. These buses had ultra-lightweight MCW Orion bodies, which led to the legendary description of them by a local politician as 'monstrous masses of shivering tin'. This 1954 example is seen in Saltcoats in June 1972 after sale to Steele, Stevenston, one of the members of the famous A1 Service co-operative. The destination, Stevenston Pillar Box, shows a degree of precision which is sometimes lacking.
Iain MacGregor

Left:
The model that completely changed all previous thoughts on double-deck design was the Leyland Atlantean, the first rear-engined double-decker. Introduced in 1958, the Atlantean sold widely during its long career, and this was typical of many early models, with fairly boxy-looking bodywork. It is a 1960 Gateshead & District PDR1/1 with Roe 78-seat body, and it is seen threading its way through the maze of bridges on the Gateshead bank of the River Tyne. Roe had normally been associated with attractive and traditionally-styled bodywork, but followed MCW's lead with designs that took little advantage of the opportunities presented.
Arnold Richardson/Photobus

Above:
Although the Scottish Bus Group companies could, and did, buy Bristol Lodekkas, some also chose to buy traditional lowbridge double-deckers. Central SMT, operating around Glasgow, took 10 of these Leyland Titan PD2/30 with Northern Counties 59-seat bodies in 1959. This one is seen in August 1963 on service to the Clyde resort of Helensburgh. Central was one of several UK fleets which changed to high-capacity 36ft single-deckers when these became available in the 1960s, and subsequent double-deck purchases, most notably Albion Lowlanders and Daimler Fleetlines, only stayed in the fleet for short periods before finding their way to other SBG companies.
D. Kerrison/Photobus

75

Above:
When 36ft single-deckers were legalised in 1961, many operators turned to them as a high-capacity (up to 55 seats) alternative to double-deckers. Farsley Omnibus of Stanningley, part of the Wallace Arnold empire from 1952, bought this Leyland Leopard PSU3/2 in 1964, fitted with a Plaxton Highway 51-seat body, to work the Pudsey-Tinshill service. It is seen in

August 1964. The Farsley business passed to Leeds City Transport in 1968.
Arnold Richardson/Photobus

Right:
Halifax Corporation buses wore a livery influenced by the striking Glasgow Corporation colours. This 1965 Leyland Titan PD2/37 had a forward entrance Weymann 64-seat body,

and was one of a batch of 10. It is seen loading in George Street, Halifax in July 1969, under a menacing sky. Several operators continued to buy shorter-length double-deckers, often with forward entrances, in preference to the 30ft buses that were available.
M. J. Russell

Left:
The driver is caught in mid-leap from the cab of a Yorkshire Traction Leyland Titan PD3A/1 with the later style of full-width bonnet, based on buses built for St Helens. New in 1963, it has Northern Counties 73-seat forward-entrance bodywork, and is seen at Barnsley bus station. Double-deckers of 30ft length with forward entrances, similar to this one, were popular with operators requiring higher seating capacities, from 1956, when two-axle double-deckers to this length were legalised, until the rear-engined double-deckers (and indeed Leyland) gained a complete monopoly around 1970.
Arnold Richardson/Photobus

Above:
One of the early attempts to improve the looks of bodywork on Leyland Atlantean chassis was this Alexander design, using curved glass and glassfibre to good effect. This style was first produced for Glasgow Corporation, but it was quickly adopted by other operators – and other bodybuilders. Newcastle Corporation was an early Atlantean customer, and went on to build up a substantial fleet. This 1965 example, with 78-seat Alexander body, is seen near Central Station in June 1965, passing a Plaxton-bodied Bedford SB.
J. T. Inglis

The 'Heyday' series from IAN ALLAN

Publishing

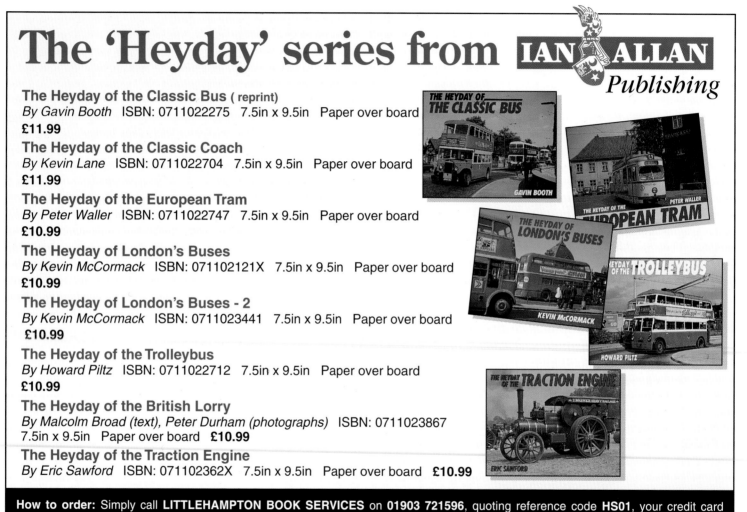

The Heyday of the Classic Bus (reprint)
By Gavin Booth ISBN: 0711022275 7.5in x 9.5in Paper over board
£11.99

The Heyday of the Classic Coach
By Kevin Lane ISBN: 0711022704 7.5in x 9.5in Paper over board
£11.99

The Heyday of the European Tram
By Peter Waller ISBN: 0711022747 7.5in x 9.5in Paper over board
£10.99

The Heyday of London's Buses
By Kevin McCormack ISBN: 071102121X 7.5in x 9.5in Paper over board
£10.99

The Heyday of London's Buses - 2
By Kevin McCormack ISBN: 0711023441 7.5in x 9.5in Paper over board
£10.99

The Heyday of the Trolleybus
By Howard Piltz ISBN: 0711022712 7.5in x 9.5in Paper over board
£10.99

The Heyday of the British Lorry
By Malcolm Broad (text), Peter Durham (photographs) ISBN: 0711023867
7.5in x 9.5in Paper over board **£10.99**

The Heyday of the Traction Engine
By Eric Sawford ISBN: 071102362X 7.5in x 9.5in Paper over board **£10.99**